Taking Food Allergies To School

By Ellen Weiner

Written for and Adapted for the
Special Kids in School Series®
Created by Kim Gosselin

Taking Food Allergies To School
Copyright © 1999, by JayJo Books, LLC.
First Edition. All rights reserved. No part of this book may be reproduced in any manner whatsoever without written permission from the publisher. For information address JayJo Books, LLC., P.O. Box 213, Valley Park, MO 63088-0213. Printed in the United States of America.

Published by
JayJo Books, LLC.
Publishing Special Books for Special Kids®
P.O. Box 213
Valley Park, MO 63088-0213
Edited by Kim Gosselin
Design by Fran Sherman

Library of Congress Cataloging-in-Publication Data
Weiner, Ellen
Taking Food Allergies to School/Ellen Weiner–First Edition
Library of Congress Catalog Card Number 99-71576
1. Juvenile/Non-Fiction
2. Health Education
3. Food Allergies

ISBN 1-891383-05-1
Library of Congress
Fifth book in our *"Special Kids in School"*® series.

Taking Food Allergies to School was written and adapted for the *"Special Kids in School"*® series created by Kim Gosselin.

*Attention schools, hospitals, organizations, HMO's, etc.: Quantity discounts are available on bulk purchases of this book for educational purposes. Custom logos and excerpts can also be created to fit your specific needs. For information please contact the publisher at 1-636-861-1331.

601978166

A Note to Parents

Jeffrey is now a 13 year old child. He was diagnosed with food allergies at the age of two. He also has grass, pollen, and drug allergies. At one point in time, the only food group from which he was able to eat was rice. Through avoidance and with the help of doctors, Jeffrey has made great strides in his health and in conquering his allergies.

People constantly remark how well adjusted he is and how he takes his food restrictions in stride. It is other people who feel bad when they learn that Jeffrey cannot eat regular pizza or birthday cake. To Jeffrey this is just a fact of life. He knows how he feels when he stays on his diet and how he feels when he does not. He much prefers the former.

Children are very intelligent and they must be given more credit for what they know. Since the time Jeffrey was very young, I discussed his food restrictions with him and why he could not eat certain things. On his own level, he understood and accepted it. It is his body, and he has the right and desire to know what is going on inside of him. A child is more willing to accept restrictions when education is given.

There are many resources available for parents of allergic children. Two groups I highly recommend are: The Food Allergy Network, 4744 Holly Avenue, Fairfax, Virginia 22030 and the Allergy/Asthma Information Association, 30 Eglinton Avenue West, Suite 750, Mississauga, Ontario, Canada L5R 3E7. Both of these groups produce and distribute newsletters and cookbooks that contain invaluable information about allergies.

Ellen Weiner

Jeffrey felt awful! His chest hurt, he couldn't breathe well, his stomach hurt and he had an itchy red rash too!!

Jeffrey wasn't really sick the way you think most people are sick. He was having a food allergy attack.

Jeffrey must have eaten something that made his body feel sick even though it wasn't.

In many ways Jeffrey is just like all of the other kids. He likes to play sports, he loves school and he has lots of fun with all the other kids.

Jeffrey doesn't look or act different than any other kid. But he is different in one very important way. When he eats certain foods, his body starts making him feel really sick.

The foods Jeffrey is most allergic to are: Things made with milk (like pizza, cheese, and ice cream), corn, strawberries, peanuts and anything made with wheat (like breads or some kinds of pizza dough).

Jeffrey didn't understand how or why these things happened to his body. He asked his mom and his doctor.

They explained that inside everyone's body are things called "white blood cells" that fight germs and help keep kids (and adults, too) from becoming sick.

These cells are like an army waiting to fight enemy germs that try to enter your body. This "army" attacks by sending out antibodies that stick to germs and kill them. That's good!

Sometimes the army gets fooled and makes a mistake. The army of white blood cells gets a wrong message and makes the antibodies anyway. These antibodies start fighting the good cells in our body instead of the bad.

Allergy antibodies stick to good cells called mast cells. Mast cells are found in your skin, nose, lungs and stomach. These are the places Jeffrey looks and feels sick whenever he eats certain foods.

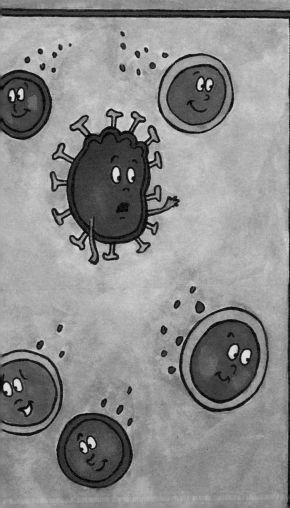

Allergy antibodies wait in our bodies until they see certain foods they do not like. When these foods go by, the antibodies reach out and grab them! This makes the mast cell explode!! The mast cell sprays out a special potion called histamine.

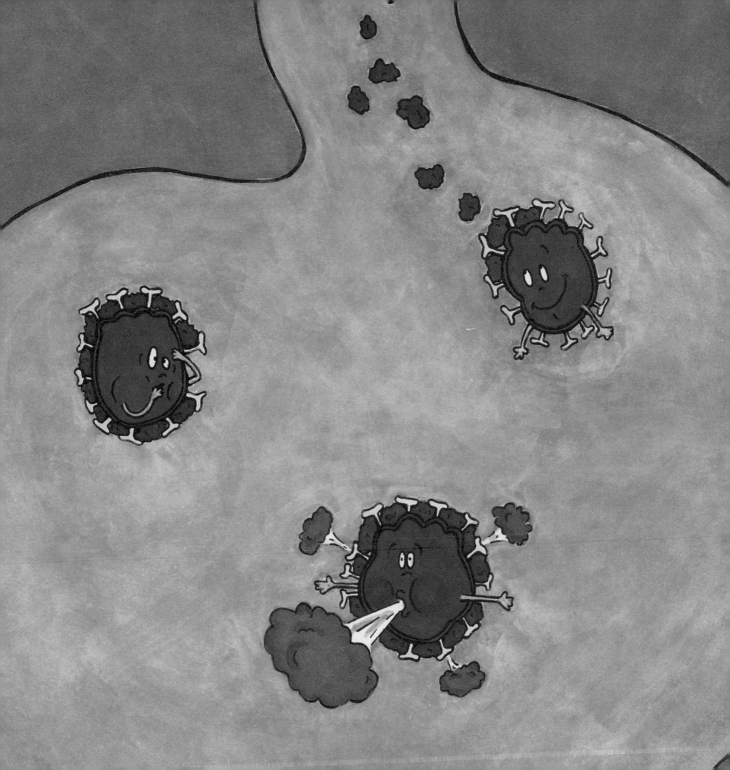

Because the food Jeffrey eats really isn't trying to hurt his body, the special potion, histamine, does not work the way it is supposed to.

Sometimes, the histamine may start causing rashes, sneezing, stomach-aches, or even breathing trouble. The histamine makes the body hurt itself. This makes Jeffrey feel really, really, bad.

Sometimes Jeffrey feels sad because he can't always share snacks at school. But his mom figured out that she can make special treats just for Jeffrey and his friends. After all, he's really no different than they are.

Jeffrey's mom even knows how to make a special pizza for him! Of course, his mom makes enough treats and pizza for all of the kids in his classroom!

The treats really don't taste any different than other ones, and the kids really like them! They just don't have the things in them that may hurt Jeffrey.

If Jeffrey isn't sure whether or not he might be allergic to something, he always knows to check with his family first.
Even if a friend or teacher says a food is okay, Jeffrey knows he can always say "no thank you."

Sometimes he even calls home from school to see if the food is okay. His teacher can help by calling his home too! Jeffrey knows how important it is to feel good!

Jeffrey's family and doctors told him that there are lots and lots of kids who are allergic to certain foods, just like he is.

Being allergic to certain foods isn't contagious! You can't "catch" food allergies from Jeffrey or anyone else. It's okay to play with Jeffrey and be his friend. He can't give you any food allergies!

What Jeffrey is most excited about is, that, as he gets older and becomes a teenager, his allergies will probably bother him less and less! Of course, there are some foods that he will always be allergic to, no matter how old he gets.

Still, there are lots of foods that he will probably be able to eat and not get sick at all; maybe even pizza! Until then, please remember, Jeffrey is a lot like you in every other way!

The End

Allergy-Free Pizza Recipe

Use ready-made pizza crusts from a health food store
 which have very few ingredients (just flour and water).
1 16 oz. can tomato sauce
1 bunch green onions
6 mushrooms, chopped
garlic to taste
basil to taste, optional
oregano to taste, optional
sugar or sugar substitute to taste
1/2 lb. ground chopped meat
2 large tomatoes, thinly sliced

1. Place tomato sauce in mixing bowl.
2. Chop onions and mushrooms and sauté.
   Drain and add to tomato sauce.
3. Add spices and mix well.
4. Sauté chopped meat until done.
   Drain and add to sauce.
5. After mixing sauce thoroughly, apply to crusts.
6. Top with thinly sliced tomatoes.
7. Bake according to crust directions.

Pizza may be eaten hot or cold.
You may substitute chicken for chopped meat.
If you wish, add other vegetables such as broccoli,
   cauliflower or diced carrots.

"Let's Take The Food Allergy Kids Quiz"

1. Name five reactions that could tell you Jeffrey is having an allergic reaction.
1) Chest hurting 2) Can't breathe well 3) Stomach-ache 4) Earache 5) Rash

2. Name three foods that are likely to cause allergies.
1) Milk 2) Corn 3) Peanuts

3. What happens when Jeffrey eats something he's allergic to?
His body receives a wrong message. The body thinks the food is something harmful so it tries to protect Jeffrey by making antibodies.

4. Why are allergy antibodies special?
They stick to special cells called mast cells. They are found in the skin, nose, lungs, and stomach.

5. When Jeffrey gets sick, what is the name of the cells that help fight the infection?
White blood cells.

6. What is the name of the special potion sprayed from the mast cells?
Histamine.

7. If a teacher or someone's mom gives Jeffrey something to eat, can he eat it without worrying?
No! He should always check the ingredients and call his family if he's not sure.

8. True or false: Jeffrey can share his snacks with his classmates, but they should not share theirs with him.
True. Jeffrey has very good snacks; they are just made with special ingredients. You might even like his more than you like yours!

9. True or false: There are very few people that have food allergies.
False. There are lots of people with food allergies. Some people are only allergic to one food. Others are allergic to many foods, like Jeffrey.

10. True or false: As Jeffrey gets older, it is possible that some of his food allergies will not bother him as much.
True. Usually, when a child becomes a teenager food allergies are not quite as bad.

Ten Tips For Teachers

1. EVERY CHILD LIVING WITH FOOD ALLERGIES IS DIFFERENT
Some children are highly allergic to one item, such as peanuts and cannot even be in the same room with the offending item. Other children may have a list of forbidden foods, but will not have a life threatening reaction if one of the items is ingested by mistake. A list of the allergic foods and the possible reaction to them should always be kept in the child's classroom and in the nurse's office so that it may be referred to if there are any questions.

2. BE AWARE OF HIDDEN INGREDIENTS FOUND IN FOODS
Always check the ingredient list. A child allergic to milk cannot have ice cream, cheeses, regular pizza or yogurt. Any item that contains whey, casein, sour cream, calcium lactate, lactose, sodium caseinate or butter is usually forbidden. A child allergic to sugar cannot have any item that contains corn syrup, dextrose, glucose, fructose or honey (all fast food french fries contain dextrose!) A child allergic to corn cannot have any item that contains caramel coloring, grits, hominy, maize, malt, sorbitol, succotash, dextrin/maltodextrin, karo, glucose or fructose.

3. LISTEN TO THE ALLERGIC CHILD
Do not push "a taste" of a food on an allergic child. Believe him/her when they say they are not allowed to have the food or if they begin to feel ill after ingestion.

4. ALWAYS BE PREPARED
Let the allergic child's family know when the class will be celebrating a birthday or any other "treat" day. Arrangements can always be made for an alternate snack for the child. Many parents with allergic children are more than happy to bring in treats for the whole class so that their child can eat what everyone else is eating.

5. ALLOW UNRESTRICTED BATHROOM BREAKS
If a child eats something they are allergic to, stomach cramps and diarrhea may result. They may not have time or be embarrassed to ask permission to visit the bathroom.

6. CONSTRUCT A UNIT ON HOW PEOPLE ARE DIFFERENT

Some people wear glasses, some have to take medicines each day, some wear braces, some are in a wheelchair, and some have restricted diets. This will allow you to point out the allergic child's problem foods without singling any specific child out. Once they are educated about the offending items, classmates tend to look out for that child. Then, there will usually be no sharing of lunches or snacks.

7. ALLOW THE ALLERGIC CHILD'S MOM/DAD TO BE THE CLASSROOM PARENT

The classroom parent(s) generally plan holiday parties and go on field trips. It makes it easier on the child, parent and the teacher if the mom/dad can carry snacks for their child so they don't feel left out on a field trip. The parent can also help in making foods or checking with other committee parents about ingredients that will not work.

8. SUBSTITUTE REWARDS FOR A JOB WELL DONE

Many teachers reward their students with candy or a pizza party. Be aware of the allergic child's limitations and plan an alternate treat or pizza for him/her. A sticker, pencil, or extra credit points instead of a piece of candy are good substitutes.

9. DO NOT FEEL SORRY FOR THE ALLERGIC CHILD

An allergic child knows how he/she feels when the right or wrong food is eaten. They will usually choose to do the right thing. They also are often eating a very healthy diet...no junk foods, no preservatives, no sugar. Their food allergies are helping them to build strong character and develop willpower which will serve them well as adults. They should be admired for their strength, not pitied for their deprivations.

10. WHEN A CLASS UNIT INCLUDES COOKING AND EATING, PLAN AN ALTERNATE ACTIVITY

This is especially important for younger children. If children are mixing ingredients to make cookies, for example, the allergic child should neither eat the finished product nor touch any of the offending ingredients. For the allergic child to participate, they might gather all the ingredient boxes together; read aloud the recipe; write the recipe on the board; cut up and distribute the finished product; etc. The child may also wear plastic gloves so the ingredients do not touch his/her skin. Everyone in the class should always wash their hands thoroughly when the activity is completed so the offending ingredient is not passed around on items the children might touch.